Dear D[...]

Happy Birthday!

Love,

Uncle Tom & Aunt Suzanne,
Timmy & Suzy

For Tom

First published 1987 by William Collins Sons & Co Ltd
London   Glasgow   Sydney   Auckland   Toronto   Johannesburg

An Albion Book

Conceived, designed and produced by The Albion Press Ltd, 9 Stewart Street, New Hinksey, Oxford OX1 4RH

Designer: Linda Sullivan

© Text: Neil Philip 1987   © Illustrations: Sarah Pooley 1987   © Volume: The Albion Press Ltd 1987

All rights reserved. No part of this publication may be reproduced, stored in a retrieval system, or transmitted, in any form or by any means, electronic, mechanical, photocopying, recording or otherwise, without the prior written permission of the copyright holders.

British Library Cataloguing in Publication Data
Philip, Neil
  Animal antics.
  1. Zoo animals——Juvenile literature
  I. Title   II. Pooley, Sarah
  590′.74′4

ISBN 0 00 184847 X

Typeset by Dentset, Oxford   Colour reproduction by Dot Gradations Ltd
Printed and bound in Great Britain by Purnell & Sons (Book Production), Bristol

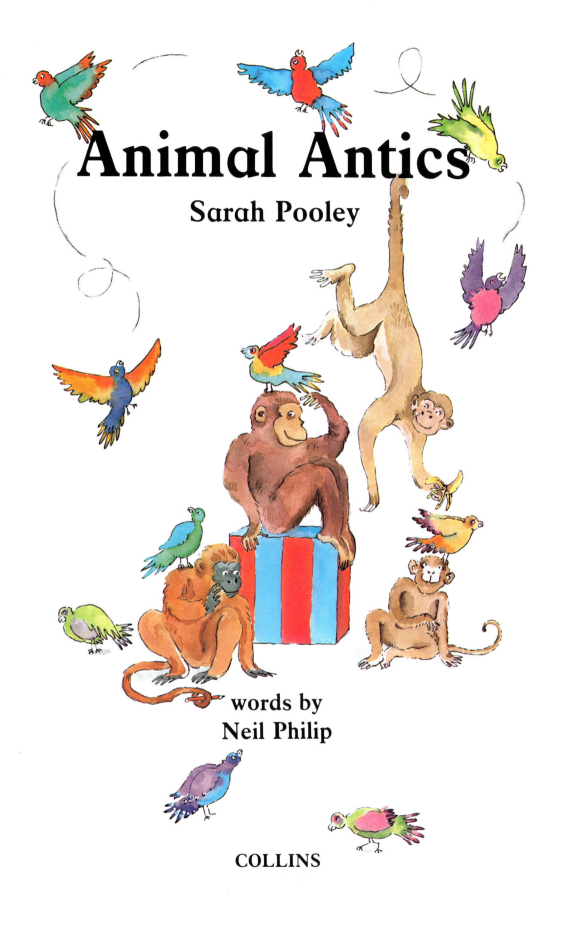

Animal Antics

Sarah Pooley

words by
Neil Philip

COLLINS

When we went to the zoo we saw

Proud peacocks preening in the park

Enormous elephants eating everything

Lazy lions licking their lips

Plump pandas peacefully pondering

Cross camels causing chaos

Flamboyant flamingoes feeling fanciful

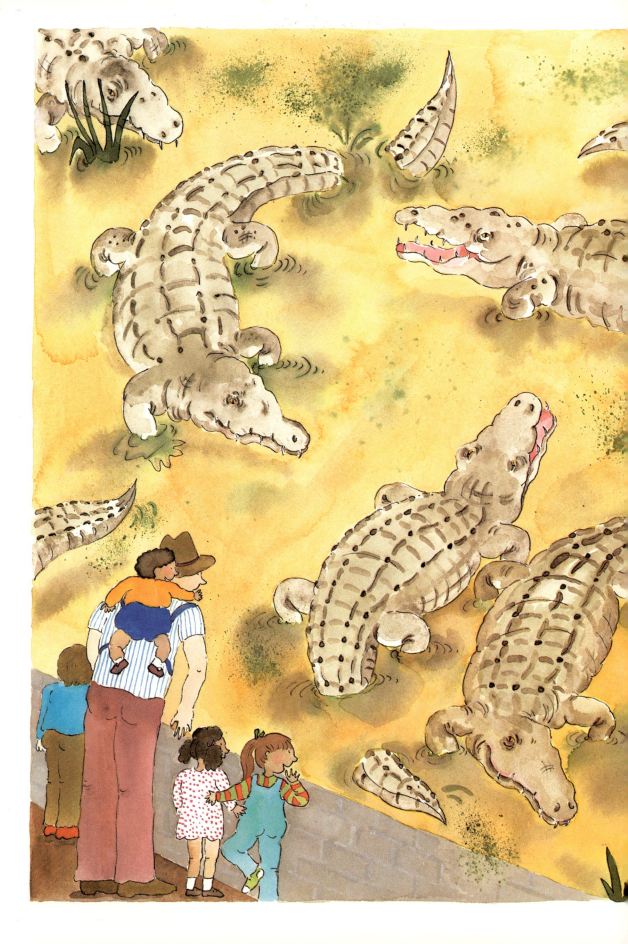

Agitated alligators alarming all and sundry

Zestful zebras zig-zagging zanily

Colourful cockatoos cawing and cackling

Perky penguins playing in a pond

Mischievous monkeys making mock

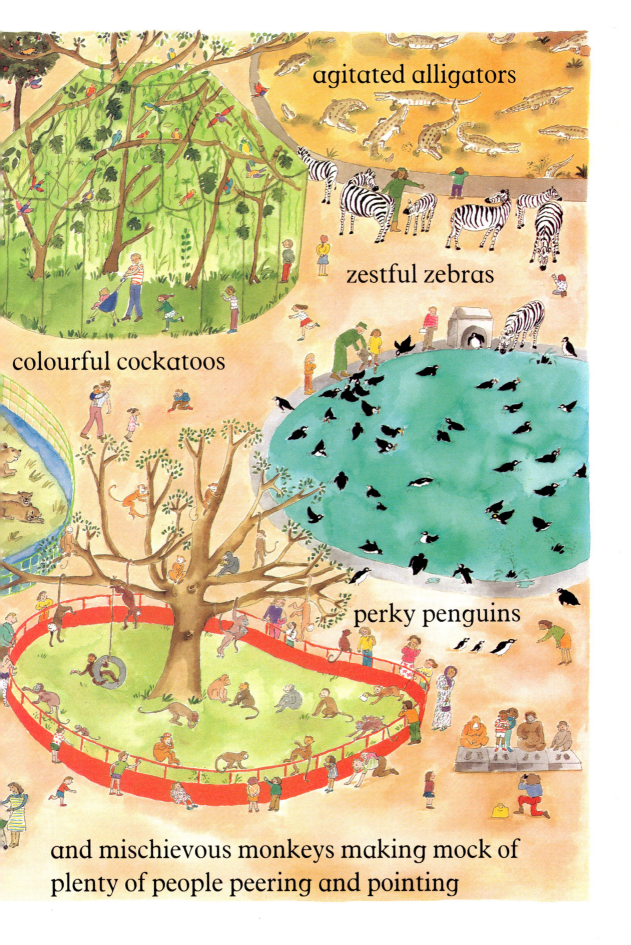